It is no use bringing a number of people
together who cannot amuse each other—
far better is it (although more trouble
perhaps) to have several little dinners
to which only kindred spirits need be
bidden, than one large one.

MRS. ISABELLA BEETON,
THE BOOK OF HOUSEHOLD MANAGEMENT,
1861.

OTHER BOOKS:

The Terrace Times
    Minimum Effort Maximum Effect
Cook Book — Paddington Edition

The Terrace Times
    Minimum Effort Maximum Effect
Cook Book — The Rocks Edition

The Terrace Times
    Minimum Effort Maximum Effect
Cook Book — Balmain Edition

The Terrace Times
    Minimum Effort Maximum Effect
Cook Book — Looking at Cooking

The Terrace Times
    Minimum Effort Maximum Effect
Cook Book — Melbourne Edition

The Terrace Times
    Minimum Effort Maximum Effect
Garden Book — The Tiny Utopia

DEDICATED TO PIPPA, BENJAMIN, TIMOTHY AND KATIE

The Sydney Harbour Bridge, which
frames the Opera House on our
cover, is the world's largest
single span arch bridge. It can
be crossed by car, train, bus,
bicycle and on foot.

Volume Six

$4.95 Recommended Retail Price

The Terrace Times
COOK BOOK
CITY OF SYDNEY EDITION

Illustrations Allan Gamble
Food Drawings Kay Stewart
Concept Text and Design Helen Arbib

INTRODUCTION

Writing and publishing The Terrace Times cook books has become such an important and happy part of my life, it is intriguing to look back to November 1975 and the first Paddington cook book, and remember being patted on the head (metaphorically speaking) and told it should at least sell there. I must admit I was not expecting much—the book was only planned as a oncer, for the sheer fun of it—but, thanks to the kindness of the media, it sold everywhere. And here I am with my sixth book and the same illogical light-hearted mixture of history and minimum effort maximum effect cookery.

We are lucky this time to have two gifted artists instead of one! Kay Stewart—who illustrated the Melbourne cook book so beautifully—is back to do the food drawings. Architect and artist Allan Gamble is responsible for the other illustrations and splendid buildings. As an artist, Allan has had one-man exhibitions in New York, Perth and Sydney, and he was, until 1972, Director of the University of Sydney's Gallery of Fine Arts.

Sydney's early history is the early history of the white man's Australia, because Sydney is where it all began in 1788. But it cannot be accompanied by the typically Australian recipes that have evolved since then, because they haven't! The Aborigine-style *bush tucker* of the first years of drought and famine was soon abandoned, and what we have is a legacy from British settlers whose diet was determinedly unaffected by their new enironment, combined with a wealth of culinary creativity and variety provided by migrants from all over the world, who have been settling here since the end of World War II. It may not be a national cuisine, but it's a fascinating mixture.

Helen Arbib

THE TERRACE TIMES PTY. LTD.,
15 ROSLYNDALE AVENUE, WOOLLAHRA, N.S.W. 2025,
AUSTRALIA

First published 1980
Concept and text © by Helen Arbib 1980
Illustrations © by Allan Gamble 1980
Food Drawings © by Kay Stewart 1980
All rights reserved
National Library of Australia card number and
ISBN 0 9598486 6 5
Wholly designed and set up in Australia
Typesetting: ASA Typesetters, Sydney
Printed by Sydney Allen Printers Pty. Ltd. Rydalmere

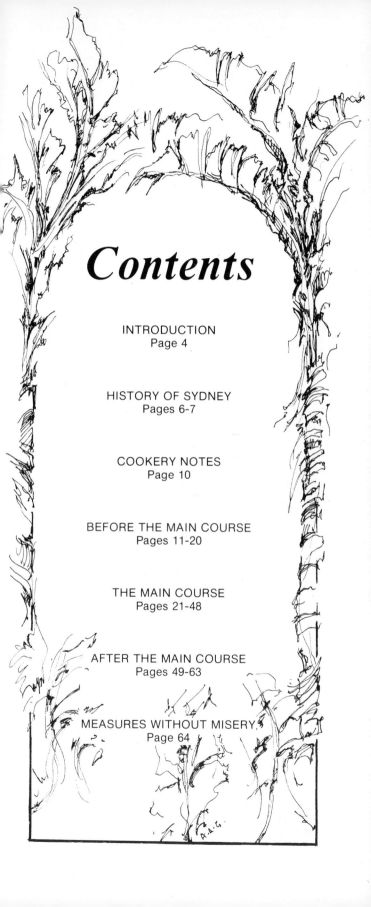

Contents

The first Europeans to land in Australia were the Dutch in 1606, but nothing was done about it, and it took the American War of Independence to make it a British Colony nearly 200 years later ... in January 1788, when Captain Arthur Phillip and the First Fleet—with its two warships *Sirius* and *Supply*—ended an eight-months voyage to unload, in Sydney Cove, their dismal cargo of convicts who could no longer be dumped on the American colonies.

They had discovered "the finest and most extensive harbour in the universe" and a cove where the ships could anchor in safety, which Phillip named for the Home Secretary, the 1st Viscount Sydney—a man called *maggot-head* by his enemies. They found a fern-decked brook (later named the Tank Stream for the reservoirs built to conserve it) and a shore bounded by rocks and mangrove trees covered in small finely-flavoured oysters. And they found small groups of Aborigines quietly watching as the white strangers moved in on their land.

The first two years were terrible years of drought and famine, with no relief from home, and it is typical of the haphazard way in which Sydney struggled and grew that it was never officially named. It was to be called *Albion*, but eventually became known for the cove where settlement was first established. They were also cruel years, with public hangings for the entertainment of the men, women and children who crowded onto rocky crags around the gaol for a good view, and no proper protection for the sick and dying under canvas. It was only Arthur Phillip's extraordinary ability and tenacity that enabled the colony to survive.

Survival was all it was. When Lachlan Macquarie—Governor from 1810 to 1821—arrived, Sydney was the seat of government, garrison headquarters, a market and a port. But it was also a disorganised settlement with delapidated buildings, almost impassable roads, and a population dispirited by poverty. He widened the streets, opened Hyde Park to the public as a common and, with convict architect Francis Greenway, created a new Sydney "in stone and spirit." But they received no recognition for it. Macquarie was condemned for extravagance and sent home. Greenway, who had made many enemies with his quick temper, was dismissed and his half-finished buildings changed and spoiled.

In the early 1800s, Sydney was still a village and every cottage had its own little garden. Escapees from the convict road gangs would hide in the scrub at Darling Point. The skyline was thick with windmills, and the Aborigines could be seen fishing around the harbour in their bark canoes, a flat stone at the bottom to hold a fire to cook their catch.

SYDNEY

Sydney became a city when the Municipal Council was established in 1842—and *males* living or working in a prescribed area qualified as citizens. But streets were still unpaved and unsewered and only an odd lamp relieved the night-time darkness. Money was short and spirits a substitute; Macquarie's hospital was built in exchange for monopoly of the rum trade. Former convicts dined at Government house and filled important jobs. Convicts serving their terms were part of a police force formed to control uncontrollable alcoholism and crime.

What a place it must have been to live in. Carts pulled by goats along the rough streets. Thousands of dogs on the prowl, biting children, frightening horses. George Street ablaze with jewellers' shops filled with loot from English robberies. Fortunes made and fortunes lost. Gracious mansions in Woolloomoolloo and crowded tenements in The Rocks.

Dates tell their own story. The whaling industry ended in the 1830s as sailing ships filled the harbour and scared the whales away. Transportation ceased in the 1840s and migrants were encouraged by a bounty system, but there was no work, and thousands of desperate people left for the Californian goldfields. The city emptied again when Australia had its own gold-rush in 1851 ... filled again as lucky prospectors returned to spend the fortunes they had made. Water was still being sold at 1d. a bucket, in 1855, from the pump in Hyde Park. Sovereigns and half-sovereigns from the Royal Mint in Macquarie Street became legal tender throughout the Empire in 1863. In the 1870s, the famous wool clippers sailed from Port Jackson and visitors were impressed by the city's political and commercial importance: in the 1880s a local paper called it "selfish and backward." It was in Sydney that the first steps were taken towards Federation in 1901.

Sydney in the 20th century had survived the crash of 1893 to become, after London, the largest city in the British Commonwealth. It was still a city of contrasts. Shops open until midnight; concerts in the new Town Hall; theatre flourishing; and hotels like Adam's and the Australia Hotel noted for their fine food and drink. But lectures by the Botanic Gardens curator cancelled because it was considered unseemly to mention the sex life of plants, and bathers caught sitting on a beach in a costume fined £25.

High-rise buildings changed the city skyline, high expectations changed its way of life, and the migrants who settled in Sydney after World War II changed it most of all. A wretched, solitary convict settlement has now become an exciting, thriving city that will celebrate, in 1988, its bi-centenary as the birthplace of Australia.

Sadly, Sydney's old and varied city terraces have been disappearing w
the speed of light. One day they are there. The next day, more or le
they're a skyscraper. So we felt we should include these Phillip St
houses for posterity, before they too are gone for ever.

GAMBLE

COOKERY NOTES

The best way to conserve energy for the nicest part of entertaining—enjoying ourselves along with everyone else—is to cook ahead as much as possible, and the recipes suggest this. But there are other ways. Never, for instance, to make bread-crumbs for only one recipe; it takes barely more time to crumb the whole loaf and freeze the rest in 1-cup lots for later. With lemons, it is easy to juice a few extra, freeze the surplus in ice-trays, and keep the cubes on hand in plastic bags. Rice can be cooked and frozen at a quiet time, to reduce cooking on a busy day. And it's madness to follow instructions to purée soup after it is cooked, when it is so much less effort to cook solid ingredients with just a little liquid until soft, process this, then add all the stock and proceed as directed.

It is also a good idea, in these days of high costs, to use a spatula to transfer food from pan or bowl—it's amazing how much food is wasted without one. But it should be rubber, as plastic is much less flexible.

Finally, a few reminders.
That the way food is presented can be as important as the food itself and there are always new attractive ideas in the food magazines.
That ovens must be preheated and it is wise to set them 10C/25F higher than needed, then reset when food—and cold air—go in.
That recipe serving-sizes are only approximate because of the variables (individual appetites, other dishes), but are planned for 6-8 people unless specified.
That, on Page 64, there are some quantity guidelines, along with a revision of the Balmain cook book's *Measures Without Misery*, designed for those of us who continue to find metric conversions a great nuisance. It should make them easier to bear.

H.A.

Before the
Main Course

"Is it not strange that so far ingenuity, universal approval, or general consensus of opinion, call it what you will, has not up till the present given us an Australian national dish? Although tea and damper instinctively arise in the mind when the matter is referred to, yet I take it that we would all repel such an accusation if levelled against us."
The Art of Living in Australia,
   Philip E. Muskett, 1893.

Appetisers

Of the many creative arts, cooking must be the most immediately rewarding. No waiting for the reviews to appear; reaction is instant and overwhelming. And there is nothing like a delicious meal to make everyone feel happy and relaxed and cared for. But the cook, too, should feel happy and relaxed—and that is what minimum effort maximum effect recipes are all about.

Kipper Pâté. Quick, easy, tasty, different.

Combine in processor or blender, or mash thoroughly with a fork
  1 200g can kipper fillets, drained
  2 tablespoons lemon juice
  ½ 300g carton sour cream
  67g melted butter or margarine
  ¼ teaspoon freshly ground black pepper
Stir in
  ½ cup fresh parsley, finely chopped.
Put in serving bowl. Cover and chill well. Serve, if possible, with fingers of hot toast.

An Unusual Scallop Appetiser.

Combine in a jar and shake well
  ¼ cup lemon juice
  ¾ cup salad oil
  ½ clove garlic, crushed
  1 teaspoon salt and ¼ teaspoon pepper
Then trim, wash, halve, and simmer 5 minutes
  450g scallops, in
  1½ cups water with ½ teaspoon salt
Drain well, and add to the dressing while still hot. Seal and chill several hours, shaking jar now and again to ensure all scallops are marinated. Serve them on toothpicks, with a small bowl of strained dressing for dunking.

"Horse-racing, dog-fighting, cock-fighting, rat-fighting and prize-fighting were all the rage. Scarcely anything else was thought of, and it was very hard for a young fellow to settle down."
MORRIS ASHER WRITING OF HIS ARRIVAL IN
SYDNEY COVE IN 1838.
SYDNEY MAIL, JULY 31, 1907.

Macaroni, in England in the 19th century, was the term for a rich, gadabout young man.

Blue Vein Ring Mousse, a beautifully textured glamorous cousin to a dip.

Soak 15 minutes
    1 teaspoon onion flakes, in
    water to cover
While flakes soak, soften
    1 envelope gelatine, in
    ¼ cup cold water, and stir until dissolved in
    ¼ cup hot water
Leave to cool and mix together
    125g Blue Vein cheese, mashed
    2 tablespoons lemon juice
    ½ cucumber, peeled, seeded, chopped
      small
    salt and freshly ground black pepper to
      taste
Drain onion. Blend into mixture with gelatine, cover and chill 30-40 minutes until it starts to thicken. Beat until thick.
    1 300ml carton cream, with a pinch of salt
Add mixture gradually and beat only long enough to blend ingredients. Spoon into 5-cup ring mould, rinsed in cold water and shaken dry. Cover and chill well. When firm, run knife round inner-outer edges and unmould on large round platter.
Press remaining half-cucumber, peeled and very thinly sliced, around outer edge of mousse. Fill centre with small water biscuits.

Mushrooms à la Grecque are equally popular as an hors d'oeuvre or as a side salad.

Combine in large saucepan, bring to the boil, and simmer gently for 3 minutes
    ½ cup each olive oil and water
    3-4 canned peeled tomatoes, drained and
      chopped
    ½ teaspoon freshly ground black pepper
    ⅛ teaspoon dried thyme
    1̂ clove garlic and 1 bay leaf, both halved
    1 tablespoon lemon juice
Then stir in gently, coating them with the liquid
    500g fresh button mushrooms, left whole
Simmer on low heat, covered, 5 minutes— stirring once or twice. Lift mushrooms into serving dish with slotted spoon. Boil liquid until reduced by one third. Remove bay leaf and garlic halves, and pour over mushrooms. Cover and chill.

Soups

There are many ways to start a meal, and soup is only one of them. But it's my favourite, all year round ... steaming and warming, with hot crusty bread in winter; cool and colourful and refreshing in summer. And soup, more than anything else, proves that, while opening cans is not cooking, a few here and there work wonders—and they can always be tucked well away before the guests arrive!

Hot Salad Soup.

Wash, shake dry, and break into small pieces
    ½ large lettuce
Put in large saucepan with
    1 cucumber, peeled, seeded and chopped
    1 capsicum, seeded and chopped
    6 shallots, trimmed and chopped
    1 420g can peeled tomatoes—broken up in saucepan—and juice
Cook covered on low heat 10 minutes or until soft. Purée in processor or blender, and reheat with
    2 large chicken stock cubes, dissolved in
    4 cups boiling water
    salt and pepper to taste
Remove from heat and stir in
    1-1½ tablespoons lemon juice
Garnish each serving with
    a small sprinkle of freshly chopped herbs.

Vegetable Consommé, a delicate fresh-tasting soup quickly made just before serving.

Top and tail and slice thinly as possible
    4 small unpeeled zucchini
Place in serving bowl or tureen. Pour over them
    1 430g can beef consommé, heated, but not boiled, with
    1 850g can unsweetened tomato juice
    1 cup dry white wine
Serve with a few zucchini slices floating in each bowl.

"Heavenly Father bless us, and keep us alive;
There's ten of us for dinner, and not enough for five."
GRACE IN AN EARLY SETTLER'S HOUSEHOLD.

"When Governor Phillip, a spare man, with a keen intelligent face, and determined look, habited in cocked hat, wig and pigtail, a red coat, velvet breeches, stockings and pumps, stood on the slope of Dawes Point, under the ensign which proudly floated in the breeze, he little thought, perhaps, that his name would be immortalised. He was lucky enough to be the first Governor, and Founder of the First Settlement of New South Wales and, as such, will always command the attention, and invite the criticisms of historians. But he was in accord with the spirit of the time, which was a brutal and cruel time."
G.B., The Melbourne Herald, mid-19th century.

Iced Chicken Soup Madras will never make Gourmet Dish of the Year, but it is a delicious standby when time and/or money are short.

First, to release flavour, soak
    1 tablespoon hot Madras curry (or a milder curry, if you wish), in
    ¼ cup warm water
Combine in saucepan over low heat
    2 440g cans cream of chicken soup (sieved to remove the meat—a dead giveaway!)
    1 300ml carton cream
    1¼ cups milk
    2 whole trimmed shallots, finely chopped curry liquid
Simmer, stirring, a few minutes. Remove from heat and add
    ¼ cup lemon juice
Chill in serving bowl. Stir, then swirl in a little chilled cream before serving.
Top each bowl with grated lemon peel that has been mixed with chopped parsley.

Pumpkin Soup is a joy to cook because the pumpkin looks after itself in the oven.

Chop into small cubes
    1kg seeded and peeled butternut pumpkin
Combine in casserole dish with
    1 420g can peeled tomatoes, sieved to remove seeds, and juice
    2 medium onions, chopped
    1 teaspoon salt and ¼ teaspoon pepper
Cover tightly and cook in 180C/350F oven 1 hour or until pumpkin is just tender. Cool, then purée briefly—so texture is not too smooth—in processor or blender.
In large saucepan, dissolve
    2 large chicken stock cubes, in
    4 cups boiling water
Stir in pumpkin and heat with
    additional salt to taste
Serve hot with a large knob of butter swirled through it with a fork, and pass the black-pepper grinder with each bowl .. the final perfect touch.

17

Crab Bisque is quite extraordinary. It is hard to believe that such a combination of cans can produce a gourmet soup to take pride of place in any company.

Combine in a large saucepan
    1 440g can tomato (not cream of) soup
    1 440g can pea and ham soup
    1 430g can beef consommé
Just before serving, and not before, heat until hot and blended. Then stir in
    pinch of mace
    1 cup cream
    1 tablespoon brandy
    1 170g can flaked crab meat
    salt to taste
Bring to boiling point and serve immediately.

Almost Instant Avgolémono Soupa. Do not be put off by the packet soup; the recipe comes from a Greek cook and is very good.

Cook according to directions
    2 packets chicken noodle soup
Reduce to minimum simmer and add
    2 tablespoons rice
    2 small chicken cubes
In a bowl, combine
    2 beaten eggs
    juice of a large lemon
Add 3-4 tablespoons hot soup to egg mixture. Return to soup. Stir in one direction only(!) as it simmers—it must not boil—until rice is cooked.

Chicken and Beef Stock. Time was when no cook worthy of the name would make soup without making stock. But today's stocks usually need cubes for flavour, so we may as well use them in the first place! For special soups, I like this compromise.

Add to 4 cups water and simmer 30 minutes
    2 large beef or chicken stock cubes
    ¼ cup each sliced onions, carrots, celery
    1 cup dry white wine and a bouquet garni
Strain and season to taste.

Sydney always had its eccentrics, not least the newspaper-seller who stood on the corner of Pitt and Park Streets in the early 1900s with a chain of chops or steaks around his neck.

Entrées

Now that pasta has been designated "up-scale" and "the Renaissance food of the 80s," with *nouvelle cuisine* no longer as *nouvelle* as it used to be, we can start to enjoy our calories again.

Pasta alla Crema is a simple dish that can be upgraded at any time with generous quantities of *fresh* mushrooms, sautéed, and small strips of fried bacon instead of the ham.

Add gradually to large pan boiling salted water
    300-500g any small pasta, with
    1 tablespoon oil
Cook, tasting, 7-10 minutes until *al dente*—floury taste gone but firm to the bite. Drain well and combine with
    1 385g can champignons in brine, drained
    1 125g packet sliced leg ham, chopped
    250g Cheddar cheese, grated
    1 300ml carton cream
    salt to taste and freshly ground pepper
Pour into buttered ovenproof dish and top with
    a generous sprinkle of parmesan
Heat, uncovered, in 180C/350F oven, 10-15 minutes until hot and bubbling.
Garnish with
    a little paprika for colour

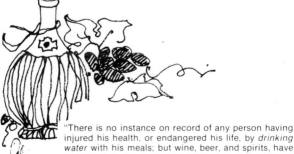

"There is no instance on record of any person having injured his health, or endangered his life, by *drinking water* with his meals; but wine, beer, and spirits, have generated a much greater number and diversity of patients, than would fill all the hospitals in the world."
THE HOUSEKEEPER'S GUIDE, 1822.

Kadin Budu is a Turkish entrée but is perfectly suitable for a main course. To save time at the last moment, it can be prepared ahead and cooked when required.

Combine and knead until smooth
125g cooked rice, with
500g lean minced lamb
1 medium onion, finely chopped
125g cottage cheese
1 egg
1 teaspoon salt and ¼ teaspoon pepper
Shape into egg-size balls, flatten slightly, and dip into
1-2 lightly beaten eggs
Coat lightly with flour and fry in olive oil until brown on all sides. Arrange in baking dish and cook uncovered in 180C/350F oven 45 minutes or until lamb is done. In Turkey, they are fried over a high heat (the oven method is easier when entertaining) and served with mashed potatoes and peas, probably followed by a main course with vegetables, cold green beans cooked in olive oil, and a sweet.

Melon, Prawns and Superlatives. A superb, easy, elegant, light start to any meal—or main dish for a few favourite people—perfect on a hot summer's day or night. Even more perfect served with well-chilled champagne.

Prepare ahead, cover, and refrigerate separately
1 cup mayonnaise (see Page 48) without garlic
500g prawns, shelled, deveined and, if large, cut into 2-3 pieces
1 medium-sized ripe but firm cantaloupe melon, with top sliced off, flesh and seeds removed, and flesh cut into small cubes and put into bowl
15 minutes before serving, combine ingredients. Add a little juice from melon cubes—not enough to make mixture runny. Pile into melon shell, drained of any accumulated juice. Sprinkle top lightly with paprika. Do not re-chill.

For households without a disposal unit, it is a good idea to put smelly food waste such as prawn shells in a sealed plastic bag in the freezer, until the garbos come around.

The
Main Course

Everyone who has the welfare of Australia and of Australians at heart must feel no little concern at that growing indifference to domestic life which is so much the characteristic of our girls ... What the result is, in too many cases—either the husband and the family suffer from the effects of bad Cookery, and unhappiness and ill-health follow, or else the bread-winner flies to alcohol in order to forget his troubles."
The Art of Living in Australia,
   Philip E. Muskett, 1893.

Fish

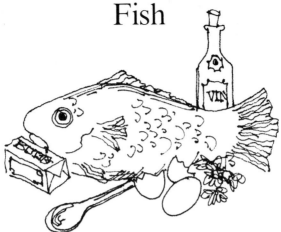

Baked Snapper with Prawns should be cooked with fish head and tail intact. If fish must be made smaller to fit baking dish, remove only tail as a first try.

Allowing 1 large fish for 6 people, 2 smaller ones for 8, have scaled, gutted and cleaned
  1 snapper approximately 1¾ kg, or
  2 snapper, approximately 1¼kg
For stuffing, sauté until golden brown
  1¼ cups fresh breadcrumbs, in
  3-4 tablespoons butter or margarine
Combine in mixing bowl with wooden spoon, or in processor (mixture is too dry for blender), until smooth with
  2 egg yolks
  3 tablespoons dry white wine
  150g green prawns when shelled, minced or very finely chopped
  ⅓ cup melted butter
  2 tablespons fresh parsley, chopped
  1 teaspoon salt
  a pinch each cayenne and powdered mace
Stuff fish cavity and secure with small skewers fixed sideways. Brush large shallow oven serving dish, or baking tin, with
  part of ⅓ cup each melted butter and oil
Place fish in dish and brush with remaining butter-oil. Cook uncovered in 190C/375F oven, basting every so often, 30-45 minutes or until fish flakes when tested with fork.
Garnish with chopped chives and serve with hot melted butter.

"The tomato, although a delicious wholesome vegetable, is not one time in a hundred more than half-cooked ... It should be cooked three hours—it cannot be cooked in one."
GODEY'S LADY'S BOOK, 1830.

NEW SOUTH WALES STATE PARLIAMENT HOUSE, MACQUARIE STREET
From 1829 to July this year, 1980, State Parliament occupied the northern block of Governor Macquarie's Rum Hospital—so-called because he allowed the contractors to import 45,000 gallons of Bengal rum, with six months' grace before they paid duty of 3s. per gallon, and with no permits issued to opposition merchants for three years. In 1843 and 1856 northern and southern wings were added, the latter a prefabricated structure imported from England as a church! Now Parliament has moved into a new building at the back of the old one, the facade of the old one is being restored, and a further building will eventually link the two.

GAMBLE.

FORT DENISON, PINCHGUT ISLAND
Rock Island was nicknamed Pinchgut by convicts banished there by Captain Phillip and fed on bread and water. The fort was named for the Governor, Sir William Denison, and built to repel a feared Russian invasion during the Crimean War. But, more than the Russians, Sir William feared "our friends, the French, and our relations, the Americans."

A Magnificent Fish Pie.

Ahead of time if you wish, sauté in saucepan until soft but not brown
> 1 small onion & 2 stalks celery, chopped, in
> 4 tablespoons butter or margarine when frothy

Remove from heat and stir in
> 4 tablespoons flour
> ½ teaspoon dry mustard
> 2 teaspoons Worcestershire sauce
> a little freshly ground black pepper

Then add gradually
> 1½ cups liquid, made up of juice from 170g can crabmeat and milk
> ¾ cup cream

Heat, stirring, until thickened and smooth, then simmer gently 2-3 minutes.

Combine in a pie dish with
> 750g any flaked cooked fish (gemfish is fine)
> 125g peeled prawns, and crab from can
> 3 hard-boiled eggs
> 3 tablespoons fresh parsley, chopped
> 3 tablespoons dry white wine
> lemon juice to taste
> freshly grated nutmeg

Cover and cool. When required, top with
> 250g shortcrust pastry, and brush with beaten egg

Cook 35-45 minutes in 220C/425F oven until pastry is golden.

Poultry

Guinea Fowl with Fruit Stuffing. A luxury dish for special occasions: for special occasions it is always a sensation. But be warned . . . the birds come with heads and feet.

Allowing 2 birds for 6 people, 3 birds for 8, thaw and decapitate, then wash and dry
    2-3 1kg guinea fowl
For stuffing 2 birds (½ as much again for 3) combine in large bowl
    300g quinces (if not available, use dried pears pre-soaked in brandy)
    250g granny smith apples
    100g onion, chopped
    100g soft butter or margarine
    5 tablespoons fresh breadcrumbs
    6 juniper berries, crushed
    3 tablespoons brandy (if using pears, include brandy from pre-soaking)
    1 teaspoon salt and ¼ teaspoon pepper
Pack tightly into birds, secure with skewers and/or thread, and place breasts up in baking dish. Brush with oil and cover breasts with
    2 rashers bacon per bird, with
    2 small pieces butter pressed into them
Add 1¼cm (½") water to pan, cover with foil, pricking it here and there so some steam escapes. Cook in 190C/375F oven 2 hours or until tender, basting occasionally. Remove foil for final 15 minutes to brown birds. Serve with pan juices, redcurrant jelly, boiled buttered potatoes, watercress or a green salad.
*For a simpler dish, omit stuffing and put in each bird
    2 tablespoons soft butter or margarine, blended with
    1 tablespoon chopped herbs
    a little salt and pepper
And add to pan juices when cooked
    2-3 tablespoons each brandy and cream.

"Some of the women (who frequented the public houses)were so saturated with rum that when they lit their pipes—all of them smoked—a thin blue flame used to come from their lips for a second or two."
AN EARLY RESIDENT OF THE ROCKS

Moroccan Chicken.

Brown in heavy pan
 2.5kg chicken pieces, preferably thighs, in
 ½ cup olive oil
Drain on paper towelling and place in
casserole dish. In remaining oil, cook until soft
 1 cup finely chopped onion
Stir in
 1 clove garlic, crushed
 1 cup finely chopped parsley
 1 teaspoon ground cinnamon
 ½ teaspoon fresh ground ginger
Add to chicken pieces, and pour over them
 4 cups chicken stock, with
 1 teaspoon salt
Cover and cook in 150C/300F oven 1½ hours or
until chicken is tender. Add
 2 tablespoons lemon juice
 1-2 cups black olives, preferably pitted and
 halved
Return to oven for 10 minutes. Serve with
boiled rice and a green salad.

Chicken Fillets with Cheese and Ham.

Beat flat until 6mm (¼") thick, then cut in half
 575g-600g chicken fillets (breasts, skinned
 and boned)
Sauté in heavy pan until lightly browned on
both sides, but not fully cooked, in
 3 tablespoons oil and 4 tablespoons butter
 or margarine
In gratin dish, approximately 30cmx5cm (12"x
2"), or shallow oven dish, arrange
 1 layer chicken fillets
 1 layer thinly sliced proscuitto or coppa—
 from 125g
 1 layer thinly sliced fresh pastorello
 cheese—from 325g
 sprinkle salt and freshly ground black
 pepper—from ½ teaspoon of each
Repeat until all ingredients are used up.
Pour over them
 1-2 tablespoons whisky
Top with
 70g grated parmesan cheese
Cook uncovered in 190C/375F oven 20 minutes
or until hot and cheese is melted and golden.

"If a lucky man, who had knocked down a dinner with his
gun, or caught a fish by angling from the rocks, invited a
neighbour to dine with him, the invitation always ran
'Bring your own bread.'"
CAPTAIN WATKIN TENCH, DESCRIBING SYDNEY'S
 FAMINE CONDITIONS DURING 1790.

MARTIN PLACE
Now a pedestrian plaza, it is dominated by the G.P.O., opened
in 1874—Governor Macquarie bought the land for the first
post office, which it replaced, for £30 and a hogshead of rum.
The tower and great clock, with its chime of five bells, were
dismantled during World War II as a safety hazard and
replaced in 1964 because of public demand.

QUEEN VICTORIA BUILDING, GEORGE STREET
Completed in 1889, in Romanesque style with crowning cupolas and an indoor pedestrian street, it was planned to replace the convict-era markets that had delighted Sydneysiders with their food stalls and pet monkeys, their flying foxes and kangaroos. But it failed as a market and has not had much success as anything else. Neglected over the years, it is being restored by the City Council.

For people who feel like I do about leftovers. Two small party dishes ... instead of tired reminders of meals gone by.

Chicken à la King.

Sauté until tender
    1 large green capsicum, finely chopped
    1 cup sliced flat mushrooms, in
    2 tablespoons butter or margarine
Remove with slotted spoon to hot plate. Stir in and cook 1-2 minutes
    2 tablespoons flour
Remove from heat and add
    1 cup chicken stock
Cook, stirring, until thickened. Add and heat
    2 cups chopped cooked chicken
    cooked mushrooms and capsicum
Remove from heat again and stir in
    2 egg yolks, beaten into
    1 cup sour cream, followed by
    1 200g can Spanish sweet red pimientos, drained—very important for flavour
    2 tablespoons sherry
    salt and pepper to taste
Reheat, but do not allow mixture to boil. It can be kept hot over, not in, boiling water.

Chicken Salad in Tomato Aspic.

Chill 5-cup ring-mould in freezer while preparing aspic. For aspic, soften
    2 tablespoons gelatine, in
    3 tablespoons water
Combine and heat
    3 cups tomato juice
    1 cup water
    1 grated onion
    1 tablespoon each sugar and vinegar
Stir in softened gelatine until dissolved. Add
    salt and pepper to taste
Pour into chilled ring-mould. Cool, then chill until set. For chicken salad filling, combine
    2 cups chopped cooked chicken
    2 chopped hard-boiled eggs
    ½ cup finely chopped celery
    1 peeled grapefruit cut into sections
    a few sliced olives and walnut pieces
    1-1½ cups egg mayonnaise (see Page 48)
Turn ring out on large round platter and pile chicken salad in the centre.
*A grated lemon and lemon juice may be substituted for the onion and vinegar.

Meat

For those of us whose incomes have not gone into orbit along with the cost of living, rising meat prices present us with three main alternatives. To give it up altogether—unthinkable for a nation that eats more of it than any other country in the world. To learn to be satisfied with smaller servings. And to balance our more extravagant recipes with those that make gourmet dishes from the less expensive cuts of meat.

Ivory Coast Beef comes from West Africa and requires very gentle cooking to retain the delicate mixture of flavours.

Cut into approximately 2½cm (1″) cubes and brown
    1¼kg—2 thick slices good stewing beef, in
    2 tablespoons each margarine and oil
Remove meat. Stir-fry until soft and golden
    2 large brown onions, sliced
    1 clove garlic, mashed
Remove from heat and stir in gradually, in order
    1½ tablespoons flour
    1½-2 tablespoons fresh curry powder
    ⅓ cup smooth peanut butter
    1 large beef stock cube, dissolved in
    1½ cups hot water
    1 340g can coconut milk
Stir over medium heat until thickened and combine with meat in covered casserole dish. Cook in 150C/300F oven 1½ hours. Then stir in gently
    1 540g can okra, with
    a little more water if stew looks too dry, or
    1-2 tablespoons cornflour dissolved in ¼
        cup water if stew is not thick enough
Continue cooking ½-1 hour until tender (this varies with meat). Reduce time slightly if cooking ahead and reheating. Serve over
    boiled rice
with side bowls as for curry.

A minor kitchen burn can be quickly soothed by rubbing it with the cut surface of a raw potato.

Fruit and Meat Loaf.

Mix well together
  1¼kg minced beef, lamb or veal
  150g dried apricots, apples, pears,
    peaches, chopped small
  1 large onion, grated or finely chopped
  2 eggs, lightly beaten with fork
  1½ tablespoons lemon juice
  2-3 tablespoons freshly chopped parsley
  1 teaspoon salt and ½ teaspoon pepper
Press into greased loaf/cake tin. Cook uncovered 1-1¼ hours in 180C/350F oven until meat is done. Drain juices. Transfer to heated dish. Serve with juices and **Piquant Sauce**.
For the sauce, stir over heat until boiling
  ¾ cup each sugar and white vinegar
  1½ cups orange juice
  2 teaspoons soy sauce
  3 teaspoons tomato sauce
Add and cook, stirring, for another 2 minutes
  2 tablespoons cornflour, blended with
  a very little water.

Swedish Frikadelle.

Mix together thoroughly in large bowl
  900g pork and veal mince
  6 tablespoons fresh breadcrumbs
  2 tablespoons grated or finely chopped
    onion
  1 cup cream
  2 teaspoons salt and ½ teaspoon white
    pepper
Shape into about 50 2½cm (1") meatballs and stack side by side so they do not stick together. Drop them gradually into large saucepan of
  2 litres boiling water
Cook 3-5 minutes, until they float. Lift out with slotted spoon and keep hot in serving dish, saving stock for **Caper Sauce**.
For sauce, melt in small saucepan
  ¼ cup butter
Remove from heat and stir in, until blended
  ¼ cup flour
Cook 1 minute on gentle heat, then stir in
  2 large chicken stock cubes, dissolved in
  3 cups stock from meatballs
Cook 2-3 minutes, stirring constantly. Add
  3 tablespoons capers, drained
Pour over meatballs and serve with noodles.

It is dangerous to refreeze thawed meat. Cook it and then refreeze it until required.

During the reign of Charles I, a live sheep was laid on a patient's bed as a cure for measles.

A Simple Lamb Curry is particularly simple if meat is boned and cubed by the butcher. A woman I know saves her butcher a serving of every special meat dish she cooks, and he makes sure she gets special meat!

Sauté in large pan until soft and golden
    1½ cups finely chopped onion, in
    ⅓ cup butter or margarine
Add and stir until no longer pink
    1.9kg leg of lamb, boned and cut into 3¾cm (1½") cubes
Transfer meat and onion to casserole dish and mix well with them
    1 large chicken stock cube, dissolved in
    1 cup hot water
    1 cup coconut milk
    3 tablespoons fresh ginger or canned green ginger, chopped
    3 tablespoons curry powder—strong or mild to taste
    1 tablespoon fresh mint leaves, chopped
    2 teaspoons salt and ½ teaspoon black pepper
Cover. Cook slowly in 180C/350F oven 2 hours or until meat is tender*. Before serving stir in
    ½ cup lime or lemon juice
    1½ cups small cubes fresh cantaloupe melon
    1 425g can mango slices, drained and chopped
Reheat gently. Do not allow to boil.
*Flavours are best if cooked a day ahead.

Pork and Mustard.

For an average-size loin of pork, combine
    1 tablespoon prepared English mustard
    2 tightly packed tablespoons brown sugar
    ½ teaspoon salt and ⅛ teaspoon pepper
Spread paste over pork and roast as usual.
*To retain the crackling, get butcher to make a flap of the skin and paste the meat under it.

STATE LIBRARY OF NEW SOUTH WALES, MACQUARIE STREET
The oldest library in Australia, it dates from 1826 when ten Sydney gentlemen met to plan a Subscription Library and Reading Room in Pitt Street—membership by ballot five guineas, annual subscription two guineas. But, several moves later, financial problems necessitated selling books and building to the Government, and in 1869 the Free Public Library of Sydney opened with 20,000 volumes. Today the rechristened State Library, with its Mitchell and Dixon collections of Australiana, has over 2 million books, microfilms, manuscripts, pictures and maps housed in its 3¼ acres of floor space.

Carbonnades Dauphine, an easy and tasty recipe that combines beef and beer, comes from the Flemish side of the Belgian family. It can be cooked ahead and reheated.

Cut 6-8 slices about 1¼cm (½") thick from
    1-1¼kg Scotch fillet
Fry briefly both sides, in large pan on high heat—a few at a time—until no longer red, in
    4 tablespoons oil
Remove meat. Stir until well coated in remaining oil
    750g brown onions, thinly sliced
Cover and cook on medium heat, stirring occasionally, 5-6 minutes until soft. Stir in
    3-4 cloves garlic, mashed
Remove from heat. Arrange half meat in oblong flameproof casserole dish with
    1 bouquet garni and 6 sprigs parsley
Cover with half onions and sprinkle lightly with
    salt and pepper
Repeat meat, onions, salt and pepper. Combine
    1 large beef stock cube, dissolved in
    1 cup boiling water, with
    1 370ml can light beer
Pour over meat and bring to simmer on stove. Cover and cook in 160C/320F oven 1-1¼ hours or until meat is just tender. Remove meat, discard bouquet garni. Strain liquid into small pan, simmer 4-5 minutes, stirring, with
    1 tablespoon cornflour, dissolved in
    1½ tablespoons red wine vinegar
    more salt and pepper if needed
Return meat to casserole, cover with onions and sauce so it will not dry out. When required, simmer only until meat is thoroughly reheated.

Roasts carve best if taken from oven 15 minutes before serving time, covered with foil, and left to contract and firm while still retaining their heat.

This copy of Florence's il Porcellino, presented to the City of Sydney by the Marchesa Fiaschi Torrigiani, stands outside Sydney Hospital in memory of two of its surgeons, her father and brother—its nose rubbed shiny by countless seekers after "good fortune".

Crusty Lamb Wellington is interestingly different from Beef Wellington and surprisingly simple.

Roast as usual on rack in 190C/375F oven 1½-2 hours, until fully cooked
    1 boned leg lamb, about 1½ kg after boning
While meat cooks, sauté until soft and golden
    1 large onion, chopped, in
    2 tablespoons oil
Add and cook, stirring, until soft
    125g mushrooms, chopped
Mash in with wooden spoon until mixture is blended
    1 tablespoon soft butter or margarine
    180g liverwurst, sliced
Set aside. For absolute minimum effort, join two 25cm (10″) squares ready-rolled puff pastry (or prepare your own, allowing double normal quantity for a pie, and roll out thinly). Let cooked lamb stand 4-5 minutes, just until cooled enough to handle. Then place it in the middle of the rolled-out pastry. Cover top and sides of the meat with mushroom and liverwurst mixture. Bring up the pastry to enclose lamb, trim off excess, brush edges with cold water and press down to seal.
Decorate if you wish with shapes cut from spare pastry. Prick pastry case here and there with fork and brush with
    1 egg, lightly beaten, or milk
Return to 190C/375F oven 25 minutes, or until pastry is golden brown. Carve thick slices vertically, and serve with mustard.

"God may send a man good meat, but the devyll may send an evyll coke to destrue it."
    BISHOP ANDREW BOORDE, 1490-1549.

CONSERVATORIUM OF MUSIC, MACQUARIE STREET
This last surviving example of Francis Greenway's Gothic designs was completed about 1820 as stables for Governor Macquarie's proposed new home. But the stables were considered recklessly extravagant and plans for Government House were forbidden. Greenway, whose death sentence for forging a client's contract to gain £250 was commuted to transportation for 14 years, was granted his emancipation by Macquarie only two years later—in 1816—and appointed Acting Colonial Architect with free rations, a house, coals, a convict servant, a horse, and a salary of 3s. a day.

Hands won't smell after cutting fish or onions if washed immediately in *cold* water. Hot water opens the pores and retains the smell.

Veal Escallops with Orange, a perfect dish for last-minute cooking.

Allowing 1 per person, cut into 3 pieces
 6-8 veal escallops
Sauté briefly on both sides, on medium heat, until no longer pink, in
 4 tablespoons butter or margarine
Remove to plate. Remove pan from heat and stir into juices
 1 large chicken stock cube, dissolved in
 2 cups water, with
 ¾ cup from 1 cup fresh orange juice
 2 tablespoons brandy
 1 teaspoon salt and ¼ teaspoon pepper
Add escallops and any juices, spoon liquid over them, bring to boil, reduce heat, and simmer covered 10 minutes.
Remove meat to plate and thicken sauce with
 2½ tablespoons cornflour, dissolved in
 remaining ¼ cup orange juice
Simmer stirring until slightly thickened. Return meat to pan and spoon sauce over it. Top with
 6-8 thin rounds from 1 large orange
 (allowing 1 per person), peeled
Cover and simmer just enough to reheat meat. Garnish with chopped chives or parsley.

Pytt-i-panna, Swedish hash.

Dice separately
 2 cups cooked roast beef
 2 cups boiled potatoes
Sauté until soft and golden
 2 onions, finely chopped, in
 2½ tablespoons butter or margarine
Remove onions. Brown potatoes and remove. Brown meat, adding more fat if necessary.
Combine ingredients and reheat gently with
 salt and pepper to taste
Arrange on heated platter and top with
 fried eggs and sliced gherkins.

Eight hours to work, eight hours to play,
Eight hours to sleep, and eight bob a day.
SLOGAN OF THE OPERATIVE STONEMASONS'
SOCIETY IN SYDNEY, WHO WON AN EIGHT-HOUR
DAY IN THE 1850s.

GOVERNMENT HOUSE, SYDNEY

Lachlan Macquarie, Governor of New South Wales from 1810 to 182
complained from his damp decaying residence in Bridge Street that "(
private Gentleman in the Colony is so Very ill Accommodated with Offic
as I am at this Moment" and commissioned architect Francis Greenway
design a "Handsome and Commodious Castellated House" in its place. B
the stables had been extravagance enough in a near-bankrupt colony, a
the plans were promptly vetoed by the Home Government. It was not ur
1845 that a new Government House, designed by London architect Edwa
Blore, was ready to be occupied by Governor George Gipps, and by eve
New South Wales Governor since then.

ST. MARY'S CATHEDRAL, CATHEDRAL STREET
William Wardell's Perpendicular Gothic structure, which replaced two earlier cathedrals destroyed by fire (the fate of many early Sydney buildings), was opened in 1882 and completed in 1928. Although Roman Catholics arrived with the First Fleet, they were forced to attend Protestant services or be flogged. After a number of priests were banished, their first Bishop was admitted in 1835 and St. Mary's Church became a Cathedral.

Vegetables

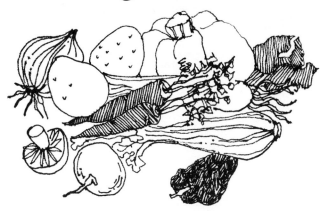

Vegetable Soufflé is really not a soufflé because it does not rise—or fall! But it contains similar ingredients and cooks in a soufflé dish. Nor, I admit, is peeling all those vegetables exactly 'minimum effort' ... but the effort *is* worth while.

Peel and cut into 1¼cm (½″) cubes
    400g potatoes
    1kg root vegetables—onions, celery,
       carrots, turnips, parsnips, swedes
Put in large saucepan with
    1 large chicken stock cube, dissolved in
    1¼ cups water
    90g melted butter
    1½ teaspoons salt and ¼ teaspoon pepper
    a bouquet garni
Cover and simmer over low heat 20-30 minutes until vegetables are just tender. Drain excess liquid, and save it for soup or sauce; it's much too good to waste. Remove bouquet garni, return vegetables to pan, and while hot, add
    1 cup cream
Leave until lukewarm, then stir in
    4 egg yolks, lightly beaten
    200g Cheddar cheese, grated
    ¼ cup fresh parsley, chopped
Beat until stiff in large bowl
    4 egg whites
Fold in vegetable mixture and transfer to large buttered soufflé dish. Top with
    1 cup fresh white breadcrumbs
Cook in 180C/350F oven 1½ hours or until set.

When potatoes were first introduced into England and Europe at the turn of the 17th century, they were regarded with great suspicion as a cause of leprosy.

An Australian 'clean potato,' was the early convict vernacular for a free man.

Hot Potatoes with Sour Cream and Dill. A Polish dish.

Parboil 5 minutes.
    1¼kg peeled potatoes
Drain and slice approximately 3mm (⅛″) thick.
Sauté until soft and golden
    300g onions, peeled and thinly sliced, in
    1 teaspoon oil and 3 tablespoons butter or
        margarine
Place in 3-litre casserole
    ⅓ cup water
    1 layer potato slices
    some sautéed onion
    a sprinkle finely chopped dill
        —from 2 tablespoons
    salt and freshly ground black pepper
        —from 1 teaspoon salt and
        ½ teaspoon pepper
    some generous spoonfuls sour cream
        —from 1 300g carton
Repeat until all ingredients are used, with potatoes on top. Cook covered 1 hour in 180C/350F oven.
*The dish may be assembled 5-6 hours in advance.

Riz au Petits Pois. If cooked rice is kept in the freezer, and cans of tiny French peas in the larder, a fancy side dish can always be produced at a moment's notice.

Cook long grain white rice in batches, the way you like best. Drain and spread out to cool quickly. Freeze in well-sealed plastic bags or boxes in 3-4-cup lots for this and other recipes. For this recipe, break up and heat
    4 cups frozen rice, in
    large pan boiling water
Immediately water returns to boil, drain rice and return to pan. Combine over gentle heat with
    2 tablespoons soft butter, then add
    1 410g can petits pois, warmed in their own
        liquor and drained
    1 tablespoon fresh chopped basil or
        ½ teaspoon dried basil
    salt and freshly ground pepper to taste.

Saffron comes from the stigmas of the autumn crocus that must be picked by hand, with an estimated 75,000 blossoms required for one pound of saffron. No wonder it is expensive!

44

ST. JAMES'S CHURCH, KING STREET
Sydney's first church was burnt down by convicts forced to attend services there. St. James's Church, opened in 1822, was originally designed as a court house by the "red-headed and terrible-tempered" Francis Greenway, who was furious when ordered to convert it. Ironically, the only known memorial to Greenway is a tablet on the north porch of the church.

SYDNEY TOWN HALL, GEORGE STREET
The first hall, now the vestibule—built, after years of protest, on the original burial ground—opened in 1874 as the Municipal Council's first home. The main "Centennial Hall" and eastern portico opened in 1889 and 1930 and house the City of Sydney Council. Before the Opera House, Sydney's concerts were held in the main hall ... no tears have been shed for the draughts, the seats, and the traffic noises!

Brandied Tomatoes.

Wash and dry
    1 punnet cherry tomatoes
Pierce hole with skewer through centre of tomatoes.
Combine
    ¼ cup brandy
    ½ cup olive oil
    2 teaspoons lemon juice
    1 tablespoon freshly chopped basil
    1 teaspoon each sugar and grated lemon
      rind
    salt to taste
Pour over tomatoes, cover, and refrigerate; they keep well for days in a sealed jar. Drain and serve garnished with
    freshly chopped chives.

It has been said that pigs resemble saints; more honoured after death than during their lifetime.

A Hungarian scientist, Dr. Albert Szent-Gyongyi, was awarded the Nobel Prize in 1937 for discovering that paprika contains more Vitamin C than any citrus fruit.

Hungarian Paprika Saláta goes well with both hot and cold dishes.

A day ahead, allowing one per person, remove seeds and pith from
    6-8 large green capsicums
Cut into strips and sauté until just soft in
    ½ cup sunflower oil
Transfer with slotted slice or spoon to serving bowl. Strain remaining oil and combine with
    3 tablespoons vinegar
    4 tablespoons fresh parsley, chopped
    1 large onion, chopped small
    2 teaspoons paprika
    1½ teaspoons salt and ¼ teaspoon pepper.
Pour over capsicums, cover and chill 24 hours.
*They keep well in a sealed jar for several days.

Italian Cauliflower Salad.

Combine in jar and shake to blend
    1 tablespoon wine vinegar
    3 tablespoons olive oil
    4-6 cloves garlic, mashed and chopped
    ½ teaspoon salt and ⅛ teaspoon pepper
Cook in boiling salt water until tender but firm
    1 medium cauliflower—a good white one
Drain and cut immediately into florets. Return to hot saucepan and add vinaigrette dressing. Arrange in serving dish and refrigerate at least 1 hour, spooning dressing over cauliflower occasionally.

Croutons add interest and texture to salads (soups too). The good thing is they can be made ahead, frozen, and heated on a biscuit tray in a 150C/300F oven when required.

Remove crusts and cut small squares from
    thick slices stale bread
Sauté or deep-fry—a few at a time—until golden, in butter-oil combined. Drain on paper towel.
*Alternatively: butter, cut, and bake on tray at 190C/375F, tossing them occasionally as they cook, to brown on all sides.

Sauces

Polish Sauce Polonaise transforms everyday vegetables such as cauliflower and brussel sprouts.

For 2 cups sauce, prepare ahead
    2 hard-boiled eggs, chopped
    3 tablespoons fresh parsley, chopped
    1 tablespoon lemon juice
Stir and cook in small saucepan until just beginning to turn brown
    2 cups fine white breadcrumbs, in
    ¾ cup melted butter
Remove from heat and stir in eggs, parsley and juice. Spoon immediately over hot vegetables, that have been drained and seasoned with salt and pepper.

Aïoli is eaten in France with salt cod, potatoes, snails, on cold meat, in hot soups. I include it for its virtuosity and as an opportunity to repeat my favourite easy mayonnaise (plus garlic) for readers without a Melbourne book.

Combine in blender or processor for 10 seconds
    1 egg, at room temperature
    3 teaspoons white wine vinegar
    ½ teaspoon salt and ¼ teaspoon pepper
    1 teaspoon dry mustard
Keep blending and add, slowly and steadily (I control it best pouring from cup into funnel)
    1 cup vegetable oil
Continue blending until mixture starts to thicken. Blend a further 15-20 seconds with
    4 large cloves garlic, finely chopped

Herb Mayonnaise is made as *aïoli*. But, when it thickens, add instead of garlic
    ½ cup finely chopped chives, parsley, and
    chervil or tarragon.

"Hunger is the best sauce in the world."
CERVANTES' HERO DON QUIXOTE, 1605-1615.

After the Main Course

Kay Stewart

"Carelessness in Cookery is just one of the rocks on which disaster occurs. An English duke, an ambassador in Paris, was desirous of giving the *corps diplomatique* the treat of a real English plum pudding. The fullest directions were given to his *chef*—all, indeed, with the exception of mentioning the pudding-cloth. When the eventful time arrived for its appearance, to his dismay several stately cooks appeared, each carrying a tureen of dark-looking fluid. The omission of the pudding-cloth was fatal."
The Art of Living in Australia,
　Philip E. Muskett, 1893.

Desserts

Entertaining and theatre have a lot in common, and there is no greater anti-climax than to ring down the curtain on a superbly cooked meal with a bought dessert, because it is "too difficult" or "it takes too long" to make one.

That's nonsense, and I can prove it! Luscious lovely home-made ice cream, for example. I only discovered how rare it is these days when I could not find extra freezing trays (I bought bar tins instead), and yet here are two recipes that are not only simple to prepare—they need no stirring while they freeze, and the lemon ice cream does not even have to be whipped.

Coffee Ice Cream.

Combine in large mixing bowl
> 2 cups cream from 2 300ml cartons
> ¾ cup sweetened condensed milk from 400g can
> a pinch of salt

Cover and refrigerate (along with beater) 1 hour. Beat until peaks form on beater, then add
> 2 tablespoons instant coffee, dissolved in 1½ tablespoons brandy

Beat until blended. Freeze in ice-trays, covered with foil, 3 hours.

*For all frozen desserts, freezer should be set at its coldest, and containers chilled in it, well ahead of time. Desserts should be transferred to refrigerator about 20 minutes before serving.

Lemon Ice Cream.

Blend well together in a bowl
> ¼ cup lemon juice, strained
> 2 teaspoons finely grated lemon peel, quite free of pith
> 1 cup castor sugar

Stir in gradually
> 2 300ml cartons cream
> a few careful drops yellow food colouring

Freeze covered at least 3 hours in ice-trays.

When ice cream was first introduced into France in the 1840s, it was said that to eat it was so good it must be a sin.

If we are ever to have a distinctively Australian cuisine, it must surely be fruit-orientated in a country blessed with such an exciting and varied supply of fruit all year round.

Khundsorov Dolma, Armenian baked apples, are cooked without their skins.

Allowing 1 per person, peel and core
    6-8 granny smith apples
Fill centres with
    1¼ cups walnut pieces from 200g packet,
      mixed with
    1 teaspoon cinnamon
    4 teaspoons sugar
Top each apple with
    1 teaspoon butter
Arrange in baking dish and pour round them
    ¾ cup sugar, dissolved in
    1½ cups water
Cook uncovered in 200C/400F oven 1½ hours, basting occasionally. Transfer to serving dish, spoon syrup over them, and let cool. Serve cold.

Golden Apple Compôte combines apple and that much neglected fruit, the quince. It was called 'golden apple' by the ancient Greeks, who treasured it as a symbol of love and happiness.

Bring to the boil, stirring until dissolved
    1 cup sugar, in
    2 cups water
Add to boiling syrup
    800g quinces, peeled, cored and sliced
    350g granny smith apples, peeled, cored
      and sliced
    2 whole cloves
    1 5cm (2") stick cinnamon
    1 tablespoon lemon juice
Reduce heat and cook gently, covered, about 7-10 minutes until fruit is tender. Serve cold with liquid cream.

"It is a great mistake for cooks to serve raw fruits to anyone, but the habit some have fallen into of letting small children eat it is nothing less than pernicious.
19TH CENTURY COOK BOOK.

THE GREAT SYNAGOGUE, ELIZABETH STREET
Designed with towered bays and intricately decorated
cupolas by Thomas Rowe, the architect who also designed
the first arcade to remove shops from choked-up streets—the
Sydney Arcade, it was consecrated in 1878. Erection of the
Synagogue was made possible by the Christian population's
generous response to a public appeal and fun fair to raise the
necessary funds.

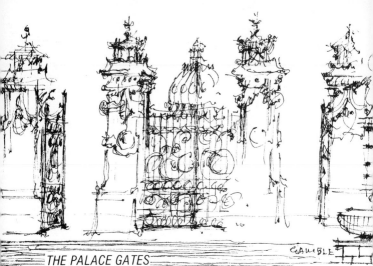

THE PALACE GATES
The Macquarie Street entrance to the Royal Botanic Gardens is all that remains of James Barnet's grand Garden Palace that housed Sydney's first International Exhibition in 1879-80. It was destroyed by a mysterious fire two years later, which also destroyed the convict records housed there. Not so mysterious after all?

Bavarian Strawberry Cheese Pie. A party spectacular.

Beat together until light and fluffy
    350g cream cheese, from foil packets
    3 tablespoons cream
easing mixture from beater and sides of bowl.
Continue beating-freeing mixture while adding
    1 400g can sweetened condensed milk
    ⅓ cup lemon juice
    ½ teaspoon vanilla essence
When well blended, pour into 25cm (10") pie dish, smooth surface, cover and chill 3-4 hours until firm. In the meantime, remove stems from
    1 punnet strawberries
Pour over them
    2 tablespoons sugar, dissolved in
    1 cup orange juice
When pie is set, drain orange juice for glaze, adding more if necessary to make 1 cup. Halve strawberries and arrange cut-side down all over pie. Stir orange juice into
    3 teaspoons cornflour
Cook, stirring all the time, until clear. Pour thinly over surface of pie and leave to set.

"Bord han Loggin here for singil ginthilmin han thei wives han childer, if so be they've got hany.—JUDITH O'CALLAGHAN.
Card in the window of a Kent Street house in 1825.

Never double salt when you double a recipe. Use half as much again and taste.

Kishmish, I'm told, means *dried fruits* in Armenian, *mixed-up* in Russian, and originated as a sweet in Persia.

Wash and soak overnight
    115g each dried figs, apricots, apple rings,
        pitted prunes and sultanas, with
    30g currants, in
    3¾ cups water
Next day, drain fruit and simmer liquid uncovered 10 minutes, with
    peel of 1 small lemon, juiced
    ½ teaspoon each nutmeg, cinnamon,
        allspice and cloves
    230g raw sugar
Remove peel. Add drained fruit and
    juice of the peeled lemon
Cook gently, uncovered, 30 minutes. Cool and add
    1½ tablespoons brandy
Serve cold with liquid cream.

Chilled Baked Pears.

Wash, dry, and place upright in a casserole dish that fits them nicely—allowing 1 per person
    6-8 ripe but firm dessert pears, with stalks
Simmer together for 5 minutes
    ¾ cup water
    ¾ cup sweet sherry
    ½ cup raw sugar
    small pieces peel from 1 orange, cut thinly
        without pith with potato peeler
Pour syrup over pears. Cover and bake in 160C/320F oven 1 hour. Leave pears in casserole dish, or transfer to a shallow bowl, and spoon syrup over them. Chill until required. Serve with
    whipped cream
and sprinkled at the very last moment with a little icing sugar from a flour or sugar shaker.
*Of course pears *may* be peeled. But the browned skin tastes delicious, and colour contrast when the pears are cut open is very attractive.

"No-one with the tastes, habits or feelings of a lady should ever come out to Australia. It may do for mediocre governesses who can put up with the roughnesses, or I should say vulgarity of mind and great want of intellect, but I would never advise a lady to try it."
LETTER FROM AN UNHAPPY NEW ARRIVAL IN 1869.

THE CLOCK TOWER, UNIVERSITY OF SYDNEY. PARRAMATTA ROAD
Australia's oldest university, founded in 1850, was created by Edmu
Blacket—who also designed St. Andrew's Cathedral—and is said to be
finest work. After World War I, a carillon was installed in the clock towe
memory of the University dead.

Payn-Pur-Dew is a 15th century classic, later called *pain perdu*, now known as French Toast. A mouth-watering way to use up stale bread.

Remove crusts from bread and dip slices in
    ½ cup each milk and cream, mixed with
    2 eggs, lightly beaten with fork
    1 teaspoon sugar and ½ teaspoon salt
Fry on both sides in generous amount of butter.
Serve hot sprinkled with
    sugar and cinnamon.

Fiji Holiday.

Allowing 1 per person, lay in fireproof dish
    6-8 firm ripe bananas, peeled
Sprinkle with
    1 cup soft brown sugar
    a pinch of salt
Dot with small spoonfuls from
    3 tablespoons soft butter or margarine
Pour over topping
    juice of ½ large lemon
    ½ cup rum mixed with ¼ cup water
Bake uncovered 1½ hours in 180C/350F oven, basting 2-3 times as sauce thickens.
Just before serving stir in
    ½ cup coconut milk

Fig or Date and Chocolate Torte was sent to me by a reader many years ago. I hope she will contact me if she sees this.

Beat until thick and stiff
    4 egg whites, with
    a pinch of salt
Stir in carefully
    ½ cup slivered almonds
    ½ cup (75g) grated dark chocolate
    ½ cup figs or dates, chopped small
Butter a 20cm (8″) springform tin, line it with buttered foil, and bake in 190C/375F oven 35-40 minutes, until skewer comes out clean. Cool in tin—and do not worry that torte falls gently as it cools. Top with
    whipped cream and grated chocolate.

HYDE PARK BARRACKS, MACQUARIE STREET
The barracks were designed by Francis Greenway to house
some 800 convicts working on building projects through the
day, until they were transferred to Cockatoo Island in 1848.
The building was recently restored and will soon open as an
Historical Museum of Fine Arts.

Fraises Romanof proves in the happiest way that a classic French dish can be prepared without a team of chefs in the kitchen.

Wash under cold water, pat dry with paper towel, and remove stems from
>   2-3 punnets strawberries, discarding any that are bruised
Place in deep bowl and pour over them
>   4½ tablespoons Cointreau
>   4½ tablespoons fresh orange juice, strained
Cover and chill well, spooning juice over berries a few times.
Just before serving, top with **Crème Chantilly**.
Beat until peaks form on beater
>   1 cup chilled cream, whipped thick, with
>   2 tablespoons castor sugar
>   ½ teaspoon vanilla sugar or essence
Pipe through icing bag with large nozzle, or swirl with fork. On the most elegant occasions, serve in a silver bowl on a bed of ice.

Pears and Blue Vein Cheese taste good together and make a noteworthy change from the usual sweet dessert.

Have ready
>   ½ cup lemon juice
Allowing 1 per person, remove centres with apple corer from
>   6-8 small ripe but firm dessert pears
Peel as thinly as possible and, using pastry brush and part of lemon juice, paint each one as peeled to prevent discolouration.
Mash together with a fork until well blended
>   200g soft Blue Vein cheese
>   100g soft butter or table margarine
>   2 tablespoons lemon juice
Fill centres of pears with mixture and roll in
>   2 200g packets crushed walnuts
Decorate with parsley sprigs for stalks. Place each one on a crisp lettuce leaf on a small plate or saucer, so as not to handle pears when serving and dislodge nuts. Chill at least 3 hours.

No Sydney book could end without Jörn Utzon's $102 million masterpiece, the Opera House on Bennelong Point. Opened by the Queen only seven years ago, in 1973, it is known world-wide and has caused more controversy than any building in our history—ever since 1957, when the design was described both as "a piece of poetry" and "a giant clam emerging from a primordial marsh on some newly discovered planet."

Good Old-Fashioned English Treacle Tart
uses golden syrup now, but the name does not change.

Line a 25cm (10″) buttered shallow pie dish with
> short-crust pastry

Refrigerate. Combine in mixing bowl
> 7 tablespoons golden syrup
> 45g soft white breadcrumbs
> 3 teaspoons lemon juice, strained
> 1 egg, lightly beaten with fork

Spoon evenly into pastry case. Make 2-4 strips with spare pastry to form lattice across pie, moistening ends with water and pressing them firmly into outside edges of case. Bake 15 minutes at 200C/400F, 15 more at 180C/350F, or until pastry is golden brown.
Serve hot or cold with custard or cream

Queen of Puddings, another old English favourite, dates back to the 19th century.

Soak
> 2 cups fine fresh breadcrumbs, in
> 4 cups milk, brought to the boil

Add to milk mixture
> 4 egg yolks, beaten with
> ½ cup sugar

Pour into a greased baking dish, set in a pan of hot water, and cook 1 hour in 180C/350F oven. Then spread with
> a thick layer of currant jelly, or favourite jam

Spread over this
> 4 egg whites, beaten until stiff with
> ½ cup sugar

Bake 10 more minutes or until meringue is pale gold. Serve hot or cold with or without cream.

Tea and Coffee

The early history of tea and coffee has not been recorded. But we are told that the Chinese philosopher Confucius, c.551-479BC, advised boiling water with tea leaves to solve pollution problems. And that coffee was discovered by a long-ago Arabian shepherd who, seeing how lively his flock became when they ate the berries, became equally lively when he tried them himself. So it is really very surprising that tea did not reach England until the first decade of the 17th century, and coffee was unknown there until a coffee house opened in Oxford in 1650.

Both have been vociferously condemned over the years. In 1674, for instance, tracts were printed to warn that the whole British race risked extinction because of coffee and, as late as the 19th century, cook book writer Annabella Plumptre informed readers that tea could cause weakness of the nerves and flabbiness of the flesh.

In Australia, we drink something like 3,200,000 cups of tea a day and, after a late start, we are also drinking quite a lot of coffee. But eighty per cent of it is instant coffee. This, apparently, is partly due to the intimidating effect of all the coffee-making equipment on the market; which is a pity, because there is nothing as good as 'real coffee' and good real coffee can be made without any equipment at all.

Heat jug as for pot of tea. Allow 1 heaped dessertspoon ground coffee per cup. Pour on boiling water. Stir well. Cover jug and let stand 3 minutes. Sprinkle a few drops cold water over top to settle grounds ... and you're in business!
* It pays to buy a little coffee at a time, so it is always fresh; to try different beans until you find the flavour you like best; to use more or less than specified quantity per cup until you get the strength that suits you.

"Never purchase canistered or bottled coffee, for in ninety-nine cases out of a hundred an additional dose of dust is made to pay for the tin or glass."
THE WIFE'S OWN BOOK OF COOKERY, 1856.

Ginger and Chocolate Clusters to serve with after-dinner coffee.

Have ready
    65g crystallized ginger (or ginger in syrup, drained) sliced crosswise very thinly
Melt over, not in, boiling water
    100g small pieces dark chocolate
When soft, stir in until well blended
    2 tablespoons sweetened condensed milk
Remove from heat, but not hot water, and add ginger slices. For style, spoon into tiny coloured foil cases. Or use two teaspoons to form small clusters on sheet of foil. Refrigerate until served.

As always, it seems a pity to say

with so much unwritten and undrawn.
As always, we hope to be back one day.

ACKNOWLEDGMENTS.
My thanks, as usual, for all the help I received from the librarians at the State and Mitchell Libraries. And for a virtually unlimited supply of newspapers and books about Sydney. It is impossible to list all those I read—only the best-remembered.
Old and New Sydney, E. Hordern & Sons, ?1882.
Old Chum, Truth, early 1900s.
Early History of the Municipal Council, C.H. Bertie, 1910.
Stories of Old Sydney, C.H. Bertie, 1911.
Francis Greenway, his Life and Times, M.H. Ellis, 1949.
Sydney, the Story of a City, M.F. Barnard, 1956.
History of Australia, M.F. Barnard, 1962.
Sydney Cove 1788, John Cobley, 1962.
Serenade to Sydney, Frank Clune, 1967.
Life in the Cities, Michael Cannon, 1975.
Sydney since the Twenties, Peter Spearitt, 1978.
The 20 Best Sights of Sydney, J. Yeomans, 1978.
Elizabeth Macquarie Her Life and Times, Lysbeth Cohen, 1979.

Measures Without Misery

Let's face it, kitchen metrics will always present problems. Because old cook books use old measures, and new books vary with countries of origin. The purpose of this page is to keep basic facts and figures on hand, to limit the problems.

Don't try to convert old favourites; most scales show ounces and grams. When you do convert recipes, remember few are so exact that small variations will spoil them. And remember, too, that while 1lb actually equals less than 450g it has been officially replaced by 500g (which is great for the food shops!), and the whole conversion structure is equally loose.

**Approved Australian Standard Measures,
using Metric Cups and Spoons.**
*Cup weights for solids are approximate only, as they vary according to ingredients.

1 teaspoon = 5g/5ml   1 tablespoon = 4 teaspoons
    (But 1 USA tablespoon = 3 teaspoons)

1oz = 1½ tablespoons = 30g/30ml
2oz = ¼ cup = 60g/60ml
4oz = ½ cup = 125g/125ml
8oz = 1 cup = ½lb = 250g/250ml = ½ USA-European pint
10oz = 1¼ cups = 300g/300ml = ½ UK-Australian pint
16oz = 2 cups = 1lb = 500g/500ml = 1 USA-European pint
20oz = 2½ cups = 600g/600ml = 1 UK-Australian pint
1000g/1000ml = 1 kilogram/1 litre

Oven Conversions, Fahrenheit and Celsius.
275F = 140C 300F = 150C 325F = 160C 350F = 180C
375F = 190C 400F = 200C 425F = 220C 450F = 230C

Kitchen Utensils, Inches and Centimetres.
½" = 1¼cm   1" = 2½cm   8" = 20cm   9" = 23cm

Suggested Quantities when shopping for a meal, to be used as guidelines only.
Raw fish: 250g per person if bought and cooked on the bone—2 fillets per person for a main course
Raw meat on the bone: no less than 250g per person unless combined with other ingredients for curry, etc.
Raw meat without bone: 125g-200g per person, again varying according to quantity of other ingredients
Uncooked rice: 1-1½ cups for 6-8 people
Uncooked pasta: 500g for 6-8 people